SO-BEP-832

STECK-VAUGHN
Vocabulary Advantage
FOR
Social Studies

Vocabulary Journal

HONK

Steck Vaughn™

A Harcourt Achieve Imprint

www.Steck-Vaughn.com
1-800-531-5015

Acknowledgements

Executive Editor   Eduardo Aparicio
Senior Editor   Victoria Davis
Design Team   Cynthia Ellis, Cynthia Hannon, Jean O'Dette
Media Researchers   Nicole Mlakar, Stephanie Arsenault
Production Team   Mychael Ferris-Pacheco, Paula Schumann,
                          Alia Hasan
Creative Team   Joan Cunningham, Alan Klemp
Illustrations   Missi Jay

Photo Credits

Page 3 ©Sandro Vannini/CORBIS; p. 5c ©Najlah Feanny/CORBIS; p. 5e ©Alex Farnsworth/The Image Works; p. 9b ©Paul Hardy/CORBIS; p. 19a ©David Ball/CORBIS; p. 19d ©Tony Freeman/PhotoEdit; p. 23b ©Araldo de Luca/CORBIS; pps.23c and 27 © Lester Lefkowitz/CORBIS; p. 29d ©Douglas Peebles/CORBIS; p. 37a ©Bryan Allen/CORBIS; p. 37e ©Bettmann/CORBIS; p. 43b ©Robert Holmes/CORBIS; p. 45c ©Bryce Flynn Photography Inc/Getty Images; p. 49d ©Gerard Rollando/Getty Images; p. 57 a and c ©Franz-Marc Frei/CORBIS; p. 67a ©Ali Meyer/CORBIS; p. 67b ©Ray Massey/Getty Images; p. 67c ©BP/Getty Images; p. 67e ©Owen Franken/CORBIS; p. 69 ©Bettmann/CORBIS; p. 71a ©The Granger Collection, NY; p. 71b ©Imagemore Co., Ltd./CORBIS; p. 71d ©Erich Lessing/Art Resource, NY; p. 73a ©Hulton-Deutsch Collection/CORBIS; p. 73b ©Swim Ink 2, LLC/CORBIS; p. 75b ©William Whitehurst/CORBIS; p.75d ©Swim Ink 2, LLC/CORBIS; p. 75e ©Bob Daemmrich/PhotoEdit; p. 77a ©Bettmann/CORBIS; p. 77b ©Sergio Pitamitz/CORBIS; p.79a ©Gianni Dagli Orti/CORBIS; p. 79b ©NMPFT/ Daily Herald Archive/SSPL/The Image Works.

Additional photography by Comstock Royalty Free, Dynamic Graphics/Liquid Library, Getty Images Royalty Free, Minnesota Historical Society, Park Street Photography, Photos.com Royalty Free, Reagan Bradshaw, and Royalty-Free/CORBIS.

Harcourt Achieve

© 2007 Harcourt Achieve Inc.
ISBN 1-4190-1929-5

Printed in the United States of America
1 2 3 4 5 6 7 8 032 12 11 10 09 08 07 06 05

Table of Contents

How to Use This Journal iv

Aa 1

Bb 5

Cc 9

Dd 19

Ee 23

Ff 29

Gg 31

Hh 35

Ii...37

Jj Kk...43

Ll..45

Mm 49

Nn Oo...55

Pp Qq 57

Rr 61

Ss 67

Tt 71

Uu...73

Vv 75

Ww 77

Xx Yy Zz..79

Other Useful Words....................................81

What's That? 84

How to Use This Journal

This journal is for you! You can use it to create your own understanding of new words. You can also use it to keep track of the words you have learned.

Step 1: Find your New Social Studies Words in the journal.
Step 2: Write a definition for each word.
Step 3: Answer the question with a full sentence.
Step 4: Write
- **synonyms** or **antonyms** of the new word.
- a word or words **related** to the new word.
- the **root**, **prefix**, or **suffix** of the new word and its **meaning**.
- **smaller words** and **word parts** that you find in the new word.
- **other meanings** and **parts of speech** of the new word.
- an **example** or **description** of the new word.
- **clue words** that help you remember what the new word means.

Step 5: Create your own definitions for the Other Useful Words.

You can also add any other new words you want to remember. And, there's space for you to draw pictures. Sometimes drawing a picture can help you remember a new word.

Have fun with your journal!

abolitionist (n.)_____

_____

_____

What are some things an **abolitionist** might do?

_____

_____

Base word and meaning_____

_____

Frederick Douglass

adapt (v.)_____

_____

_____

What would you have to **adapt** to in a new

place?_____

_____

_____

Related words_____

_____

Aa

agriculture (n.)_____

_____

_____

What are some products of **agriculture**?_____

_____

_____

_____

Means the same as_____

_____

amendment (n.)_____

_____

_____

Where could you find an **amendment**?_____

_____

_____

_____

Clue words_____

_____

Aa

ancestor (n.)_____

_____

_____

How can you learn about your **ancestors**?_____

_____

_____

_____

Clue words_____

_____

artifact (n.)_____

_____

_____

What can you learn from an **artifact**?_____

_____

_____

_____

Examples_____

_____

3

Aa

agriculture

ballot (n.)_____

_____

_____

What do you do with a **ballot**?_____

_____

_____

_____

Describe_____

_____

barter (v.)_____

_____

_____

What things have you **bartered** with your

friends?_____

_____

_____

Means the same as_____

_____

Bb

belief (n.)_____

_____

_____

Name a **belief** that is important to you._____

_____

_____

_____

Related words_____

_____

border (n.)_____

_____

_____

What countries share **borders** with the United

States?_____

_____

_____

Means the same as_____

_____

Bb

boundary (n.)_____

_____

_____

What are the **boundaries** of your neighborhood?

_____

_____

_____

Means the same as_____

_____

boycott (v.)_____

_____

_____

What would make you **boycott** a business?_____

_____

_____

_____

Other meanings and parts of speech_____

_____

Bb

budget (n.)_____

_____

_____

How would you make a **budget** to save money

to buy a bike?_____

_____

_____

Other meanings and parts of speech_____

_____

_____

_____

_____

_____

_____

_____

_____

_____

_____

canal (n.)_____
_____
_____

What can a **canal** be used for?_____
_____
_____
_____

Describe_____
_____

capital (n.)_____
_____
_____

What do you need **capital** for?_____
_____
_____
_____

Other meanings and parts of speech_____
_____

Cc

census (n.)_____

_____

_____

How can **census** information be used?_____

_____

_____

_____

Clue words_____

_____

century (n.)_____

_____

_____

In what **century** were you born?_____

_____

_____

_____

Root word and meaning_____

_____

Cc

citizen (n.)_____

_____

_____

What things should a **citizen** do?_____

_____

_____

_____

Related words_____

_____

civilization (n.)_____

_____

_____

What would you want to have in a perfect
civilization?_____

_____

_____

Suffix and meaning_____

_____

11

Cc

climate (n.)_____

_____

_____

Describe the **climate** of the place you live._____

_____

_____

_____

Means the same as_____

_____

colony (n.)_____

_____

_____

Name a country that built a **colony** in North

America._____

_____

_____

Related words_____

_____

Cc

community (n.)_____

_____

_____

Describe your **community**._____

_____

_____

_____

Clue words_____

_____

compass (n.)_____

_____

_____

What tasks do you need a **compass** for?_____

_____

_____

_____

Describe_____

_____

13

Cc

compromise (n.)_____

_____

_____

Describe a **compromise** you made with a friend.

_____

_____

_____

Other meanings and parts of speech_____

_____

confederacy (n.)_____

_____

_____

Name a state that belonged to the **Confederacy**
during the Civil War._____

_____

_____

Related words_____

_____

Cc

Aa
Bb
Cc
Dd
Ee
Ff
Gg
Hh
Ii
Jj
Kk
Ll
Mm
Nn
Oo
Pp
Qq
Rr
Ss
Tt
Uu
Vv
Ww
Xx
Yy
Zz

congress (n.)_____

_____

_____

What does a **congress** do?_____

_____

_____

_____

Means the same as_____

_____

constitution (n.)_____

_____

_____

Why does your state have a **constitution**?_____

_____

_____

_____

Clue words_____

_____

Cc

consumer (n.)_____

_____

_____

What makes you a **consumer**?_____

_____

_____

_____

Suffix and meaning_____

_____

continent (n.)_____

_____

_____

What **continent** do you live on?_____

_____

_____

_____

Related words_____

_____

Cc

culture (n.)_____

_____

_____

What **cultures** have you learned about in school?

_____

_____

_____

Related words_____

_____

custom (n.)_____

_____

_____

What **customs** do you have in your family?_____

_____

_____

_____

Other meanings and parts of speech_____

_____

Cc

canal

debt (n.)_____

_____

_____

What should you do if you have a **debt**?_____

_____

_____

_____

Means the opposite of_____

_____

decade (n.)_____

_____

_____

In which **decade** were you born?_____

_____

_____

_____

Root word and meaning_____

_____

Dd

declaration (n.)_____

_____

_____

Why might someone make a **declaration**?_____

_____

_____

_____

Base word and meaning_____

_____

demand (n.)_____

_____

_____

What is there a **demand** for in your classroom?

_____

_____

_____

Other meanings and parts of speech_____

_____

Dd

democracy (n.)_____

_____

_____

What are people able to do in a **democracy**?____

_____

_____

_____

Related words_____

_____

diverse (adj.)_____

_____

_____

What makes your school **diverse**?_____

_____

_____

_____

Means the same as_____

_____

Dd

document (n.)_____

_____

_____

What **documents** do you read in school?_____

_____

_____

_____

Examples_____

_____

drought (n.)_____

_____

_____

What happens to plants and animals during a

drought?_____

_____

_____

Describe_____

_____

economy (n.)_____

_____

_____

How does the **economy** affect your life?_____

_____

_____

_____

Related words_____

_____

election (n.)_____

_____

_____

Why do people hold **elections**?_____

_____

_____

_____

Related words_____

_____

Ee

elevation (n.)_____

_____

_____

How can you measure **elevation**?_____

_____

_____

_____

Means the same as_____

_____

environment (n.)_____

_____

_____

Describe the **environment** in which you live.

_____

_____

_____

Suffix and meaning_____

_____

Ee

equator (n.)_____

_____

_____

What would it be like to live on the **equator**?

_____

_____

_____

Root word and meaning_____

_____

ethnicity (n.)_____

_____

_____

What **ethnicity** is your favorite food from?

_____

_____

_____

Related words_____

_____

Ee

executive (adj.)_____
_____
_____

What should someone in an **executive** job be
good at?_____
_____
_____

Other meanings and parts of speech_____
_____

expansion (n.)_____
_____
_____

What problems can the **expansion** of a city
cause?_____
_____
_____

Related words_____
_____

Ee

export (v.)_____

_____

_____

What are some things that can be **exported**?

_____

_____

_____

Prefix and meaning_____

_____

_____

_____

_____

_____

_____

_____

_____

_____

_____

_____

_____

27

Ee

empire

factory (n.)_____
_____
_____

What things would you find in a **factory**?_____
_____
_____
_____

Clue words_____
_____

federal (adj.)_____
_____
_____

Who is in charge of the **federal** government?

_____
_____
_____

Clue words_____
_____

Ff

fertile (adj.)_____
_____
_____

Why does a farmer need **fertile** soil?_____
_____
_____

Means the opposite of_____
_____

freedom (n.)_____
_____
_____

What **freedom** would you miss most if it were
taken away?_____
_____
_____

Related words_____
_____
_____

generation (n.)_____

_____

_____

How many **generations** are in your family?_____

_____

_____

_____

Clue words_____

_____

geography (n.)_____

_____

_____

What do you learn about in **geography**?_____

_____

_____

_____

Related words_____

_____

Gg

government (n.)_____
_____
_____

What decisions does a **government** make?_____
_____
_____
_____

Base word and meaning_____
_____

graph (n.)_____
_____
_____

What information can you place on a **graph**?___
_____
_____
_____

Other meanings and parts of speech_____
_____

Gg

Aa
Bb
Cc
Dd
Ee
Ff
Gg
Hh
Ii
Jj
Kk
Ll
Mm
Nn
Oo
Pp
Qq
Rr
Ss
Tt
Uu
Vv
Ww
Xx
Yy
Zz

grassland (n.)_____

_____

_____

What animals might live in the **grassland**?_____

_____

_____

_____

Base words and meanings_____

_____

_____

_____

_____

_____

_____

_____

_____

_____

Gg

Draw it!

Hh

Aa
Bb
Cc
Dd
Ee
Ff
Gg
Hh
Ii
Jj
Kk
Ll
Mm
Nn
Oo
Pp
Qq
Rr
Ss
Tt
Uu
Vv
Ww
Xx
Yy
Zz

hemisphere (n.)_____

_____

_____

Which **hemisphere** do you live in?_____

_____

_____

_____

Root word and meaning_____

_____

heritage (n.)_____

_____

_____

How does your family celebrate its **heritage**?____

_____

_____

_____

Means the same as_____

_____

Hh

history (n.)_____

_____

_____

How can you learn about your family's **history**?

_____

_____

_____

Related words_____

_____

_____

_____

_____

_____

_____

_____

_____

_____

_____

immigration (n.)_____

_____

_____

How does **immigration** change a country?_____

_____

_____

_____

Prefix and meaning_____

_____

import (v.)_____

_____

_____

Why would a country **import** certain things?____

_____

_____

_____

Prefix and meaning_____

_____

37

Ii

independence (n.)_____
_____
_____

How do you show your **independence**?_____
_____
_____
_____

Related words_____
_____

industry (n.)_____
_____
_____

What is the main **industry** of your state?_____
_____
_____
_____

Related words_____
_____

Ii

inflation (n.)_____

_____

_____

How does **inflation** affect your life?_____

_____

_____

_____

Base word and meaning_____

_____

interdependent (adj.)_____

_____

_____

Name two things that are **interdependent**.____

_____

_____

_____

Prefix and meaning_____

_____

Ii

invent (v.)_____

_____

_____

What would you like to **invent** someday?_____

_____

_____

_____

Related words_____

_____

invest (v.)_____

_____

_____

Why do people **invest** their money?_____

_____

_____

_____

Means the same as_____

_____

Ii

irrigation (n.)_____

_____

_____

How does **irrigation** help farmers?_____

_____

_____

_____

Clue words_____

_____

_____

_____

_____

_____

_____

_____

_____

Ii

irrigation

42

judicial (adj.)_____

_____

_____

What does someone in a **judicial** job do?_____

_____

_____

_____

Related words_____

_____

_____

_____

_____

_____

_____

_____

_____

_____

_____

Jj Kk

justice

labor (n.)_____

_____

_____

What **labor** do you do every day?_____

_____

_____

_____

Other meanings and parts of speech_____

_____

latitude (n.)_____

_____

_____

How is **latitude** shown on a map?_____

_____

_____

_____

Clue words_____

_____

Ll

legislative (adj.)_____
_____
_____

What does someone in a **legislative** job do?_____
_____
_____
_____

Related words_____
_____

liberty (n.)_____
_____
_____

How do you celebrate your **liberty**?_____
_____
_____
_____

Examples_____
_____

Ll

longitude (n.)_____
_____
_____

How is **longitude** shown on a map?_____
_____
_____
_____

Clue words_____
_____
_____
_____
_____
_____
_____
_____
_____
_____
_____
_____

Ll

moo who?

livestock

Mm

Aa
Bb
Cc
Dd
Ee
Ff
Gg
Hh
Ii
Jj
Kk
Ll
Mm
Nn
Oo
Pp
Qq
Rr
Ss
Tt
Uu
Vv
Ww
Xx
Yy
Zz

mainland (n.)_____

_____

_____

Do you live on an island or the **mainland**?_____

_____

_____

_____

Base words and meanings_____

_____

manufacture (v.)_____

_____

_____

Name some things that are **manufactured**._____

_____

_____

_____

Means the same as_____

_____

Mm

market (n.)_____

_____

_____

What is there a **market** for in your school? _____

_____

_____

_____

Other meanings and parts of speech_____

_____

mass production (n.)_____

_____

_____

Why are some things **mass produced**?_____

_____

_____

_____

Related words_____

_____

Mm

Aa
Bb
Cc
Dd
Ee
Ff
Gg
Hh
Ii
Jj
Kk
Ll
Mm
Nn
Oo
Pp
Qq
Rr
Ss
Tt
Uu
Vv
Ww
Xx
Yy
Zz

merchant (n.)_____

_____

_____

If you were a **merchant** what would you sell?

_____

_____

Related words_____

_____

meridian (n.)_____

_____

_____

How is a **meridian** shown on a map?_____

_____

_____

_____

Clue words_____

_____

_____

Mm

metropolitan (adj.)_____

_____

_____

What is the nearest **metropolitan** area to you?

_____

_____

_____

Clue words_____

_____

migrate (v.)_____

_____

_____

Why might people **migrate** to a new place?_____

_____

_____

_____

Related words_____

_____

Mm

monarchy (n.)_____

_____

_____

Do people choose their leaders in a **monarchy**?

_____

_____

_____

Examples_____

Mm

_____

_____

_____

_____

_____

_____

_____

_____

_____

Mm

metropolitan

nation (n.)_____

_____

_____

What **nation** do you live in?_____

_____

_____

_____

Related words_____

_____

native (adj.)_____

_____

_____

What is your parents' **native** country?_____

_____

_____

_____

Other meanings and parts of speech_____

_____

Nn Oo

nomad (n.)_____

_____

_____

Why do **nomads** move from place to place?_____

_____

_____

_____

Means the same as_____

_____

_____

_____

_____

_____

_____

_____

_____

_____

Draw it!

pioneer (n.)_____

_____

_____

Why might a **pioneer** move to new lands?_____

_____

_____

_____

Means the same as_____

_____

plantation (n.)_____

_____

_____

What things are grown on **plantations**?_____

_____

_____

_____

Suffix and meaning_____

_____

Pp Qq

population (n.)_____
_____
_____

How could you measure the **population** of your neighborhood?_____
_____
_____

Related words_____
_____

product (n.)_____
_____
_____

What **products** can you buy at a supermarket?
_____
_____
_____

Means the same as_____
_____

Pp Qq

profit (n.)_____

_____

_____

Why do people want to make a **profit** when they sell things?_____

_____

_____

Other meanings and parts of speech_____

_____

progress (n.)_____

_____

_____

How do you measure your **progress** in school?

_____

_____

_____

Means the opposite of_____

_____

Pp Qq

public (adj.)_____

_____

_____

What are some **public** places in your town?_____

_____

_____

Other meanings and parts of speech_____

_____

_____

_____

_____

_____

_____

_____

_____

_____

_____

Rr

rain forest (n.)_____

_____

_____

What kinds of plants might live in a **rain forest**?

_____

_____

_____

Base word and meaning_____

_____

rebellion (n.)_____

_____

_____

What event could cause a **rebellion**?_____

_____

_____

_____

Related words_____

_____

61

Rr

region (n.)_____

_____

_____

What **region** of the country do you live in?_____

_____

_____

_____

Means the same as_____

_____

representative (n.)_____

_____

_____

Who would you choose as a **representative** for

your school?_____

_____

_____

Related words_____

_____

Rr

republic (n.)_____

_____

_____

What makes a country a **republic**?_____

_____

_____

_____

Clue words_____

_____

resource (n.)_____

_____

_____

Why do **resources** need to be protected?_____

_____

_____

_____

Examples_____

_____

Rr

responsibilities (n.)_____

_____

_____

What are some of your **responsibilities** at home?

_____

_____

_____

Means the same as_____

_____

revolution (n.)_____

_____

_____

What changes might a **revolution** bring?_____

_____

_____

_____

Related words_____

_____

Rr

Aa
Bb
Cc
Dd
Ee
Ff
Gg
Hh
Ii
Jj
Kk
Ll
Mm
Nn
Oo
Pp
Qq
Rr
Ss
Tt
Uu
Vv
Ww
Xx
Yy
Zz

rights (n.)_____

_____

_____

What **rights** do people in the United States have?

_____

_____

_____

Other meanings and parts of speech_____

_____

rural (adj.)_____

_____

_____

What would you see in a **rural** area?_____

_____

_____

_____

Means the opposite of_____

_____

65

Rr

rain forest

Ss

scale (n.)_____

_____

_____

What can you use a map **scale** for?_____

_____

_____

_____

Other meanings and parts of speech_____

_____

scarcity (n.)_____

_____

_____

What problems can a **scarcity** of food cause?

_____   _____

_____

_____

Means the opposite of_____

_____

Ss

secede (v.)_____

_____

_____

Why would a state want to **secede** from the rest
of the country?_____

_____

_____

Means the same as_____

_____

senate (n.)_____

_____

_____

What job does the **senate** do?_____

_____

_____

_____

Related words_____

_____

Ss

slavery (n.)_____

_____

_____

What does **slavery** take from people?_____

_____

_____

Clue words_____

_____

society (n.)_____

_____

_____

How can people get along together in **society**?

_____

_____

_____

Related words_____

_____

Ss

supply (n.)_____
_____
_____

What does your family always keep a **supply** of?
_____
_____
_____

Other meanings and parts of speech_____
_____

surplus (n.)_____
_____
_____

What would you do if you had a **surplus** of
games?_____
_____
_____

Means the opposite of_____
_____

technology (n.)_____
_____
_____

What **technology** do you use at school?_____
_____
_____
_____

Examples_____
_____

tradition (n.)_____
_____
_____

What **traditions** do you share with your family?
_____
_____
_____

Means the same as_____
_____

Tt

treaty (n.)_____

_____

_____

What does a **treaty** do?_____

_____

_____

_____

Clue words_____

_____

_____

_____

_____

_____

_____

_____

_____

_____

_____

union (n.)_____
_____
_____

Why might people form a **union**?_____
_____
_____
_____

Means the opposite of_____
_____

urban (adj.)_____
_____
_____

What could you see in an **urban** area?_____
_____
_____
_____

Describe_____
_____

Uu

Draw it!

veto (v.)_____

_____

_____

What rule would you like to **veto**?_____

_____

_____

_____

Other meanings and parts of speech_____

_____

vote (v.)_____

_____

_____

How do people **vote** on their leaders?_____

_____

_____

_____

Other meanings and parts of speech_____

_____

Vv

volcano

wetland (n.)_____

_____

_____

What plants and animals might live in a **wetland**?

_____

_____

_____

Base word and meaning_____

_____

_____

_____

_____

_____

_____

_____

_____

_____

_____

Ww

Draw it!

Xx Yy Zz

Xx Yy Zz

Draw it!

Other Useful Words

according (to)_____

_____

apply_____

_____

argue_____

_____

cause_____

_____

collect_____

_____

compare_____

_____

conclude_____

_____

defend_____

_____

describe_____

_____

develop_____

_____

discover_____

_____

examine_____

_____

example_____

_____

explain_____

_____

explore_____

_____

identify_____

_____

imagine_____

_____

introduce_____

_____

locate_____

_____

notice_____

_____

outline_____

_____

pattern_____

_____

persuade_____

_____

recall_____

_____

report_____

_____

solve_____

_____

suggest_____

_____

support_____

_____

time line_____

_____

trace_____

_____

What's That?

Have you been wondering what's in those pictures at the top of each letter's first page? Here's a list! Look at the pictures again and discuss these questions with a partner:

- How are these things connected to the social studies words I've learned?
- What other names could you give these pictures?

Aa	abolitionist, artifact, ancient Buddha, agriculture
Bb	ballot box, bridge, boycott, budget
Cc	Constitution, culture, compass, canal
Dd	dam, documents, desert, decade
Ee	economy, emperor, exports, empire
Ff	factory, flags, federal, food
Gg	gold, globe, grassland, gargoyle
Hh	hemisphere, heritage, hieroglyph, history
Ii	inflation, immigration, Independence Day, irrigation
JjKk	justice, King Tutankhamun
Ll	laborer, Statue of Liberty, location, livestock
Mm	mask, mission, metropolitan, mummy
NnOo	nomad, Oregon Trail marker
PpQq	plantation, Queen Elizabeth II
Rr	rain forest, rural, resource, Paul Revere
Ss	scribe, slavery, spices, striking worker
Tt	tax stamp, temple, time, treaty
Uu	U-boat, Uncle Sam, uniform, urban
Vv	veto, vote, volcano, victory poster
Ww	wall painting, weaver
XxYyZz	year, zeppelin